VOLUNTEER MAGNETISM

Becoming a leader who attracts, recruits, and retains passionate volunteers

Anne Bosarge

"MAKE YOUR LIGHT SHINE, SO THAT OTHERS WILL SEE THE GOOD THAT YOU DO AND WILL PRAISE YOUR FATHER IN HEAVEN."

- MATTHEW 5:16

TABLE OF CONTENTS

Introduction	p. 5
Using this Guide	p. 9
Week 1 Introduction	p. 10
Day 1- It Starts with Love	p. 12
Day 2- Is "It" in You?	p. 14
Day 3- Work Ethic	p. 16
Day 4- Peace Under Pressure	p. 18
Day 5- People Pleasers	p. 21
Day 6- Courageous Goals	p. 24
Day 7- Rest and Reflect	p. 27
Week 2 Introduction	p. 28
Day 8- Refine Your Vision	p. 29
Day 9- A Place for Everyone	p. 32
Day 10- Never Alone	p. 35
Day 11- How to Fish	p. 38
Day 12- Training and Equipping	p. 41
Day 13- Limitations or Creative Opportunities?	p. 43
Day 14- Rest and Reflect	p. 46

Week 3 Introduction	p. 47
Day 15- Get Personal	p. 48
Day 16- Appreciate, Appreciate, Appreciate	p. 50
Day 17- Building Team Spirit	p. 52
Day 18- Flexibility	p. 55
Day 19- Lighten Up!	P. 60
Day 20- Divide and Conquer	p. 62
Day 21- Rest and Reflect	p. 64
Congratulations!	P. 65

INTRODUCTION

We ask, we beg, we plead, we cast vision, we explain, we smile, we laugh, we cry, we cajole, and... sometimes we resort to guilt. It never seems to be enough. We always need more. Volunteers... they make our world go 'round or come crashing down. What if you stopped the crazy cycle of begging and pleading? What if your ministry was so volunteer-focused that people were naturally attracted to serving? Does it sound like a dream? Too good to be true? With a shift in approach, your ministry can become a place where people are drawn to serve.

My Experience

I've been in ministry for ten years now and have been blessed with leading large, successful teams of volunteers.

- 175 volunteers currently serve in our children's ministry each month
- 150 volunteers serve 300 kids each summer at our "Camp" experiences (our version of VBS)
- Over 50 different people helped renovate our children's environments over the last several years
- We have 375 volunteers currently serving in a dozen different ministries spread out over 4 different service times

Our children's ministry volunteers wear funny hats, ridiculous buttons, sandwich boards, and matching t-shirts whenever I ask them to. Summer camp volunteers want to know the dates for next year's camp before the current camp is even over! I'm not tooting my own horn. I want you to know this strategy works.

About four years ago I began to mentor church leaders and was asked to help them build a solid foundation for successful volunteer ministries in their own churches. I modeled out-of-the-box thinking, provided them with great tools for choosing the right structure and programs, and encouraged them to be unique in their approach to ministry. I provided training on how to appreciate volunteers and craft the perfect recruiting approach with just the right mix of humor and vision. Great reports came back on how they were able to effectively implement the program suggestions and how new and revitalized ministries were thriving in their children's worship environments. But they were resoundingly frustrated that the strategies I gave them to recruit volunteers just didn't seem to be working. They weren't getting the same results I was getting at my church. So I listened to their frustrations and thoughtfully gave them more strategies, t-shirt ideas, and scheduling suggestions. Their response was continued frustration. And that's when I got frustrated.

I was missing something in my communication. I began to think about the foundational elements of our successful volunteer ministry. Why were volunteers constantly asking to join our ministries? Why were they willing to do the crazy things I asked of them? Why were they so eager, so energetic, and so excited about what was happening?

I wrestled with these questions for months before God opened my eyes. It wasn't the t-shirts I gave them or the crazy hats they wore. It wasn't about the cute advertisement during the service or the creative way I let people know about ministry opportunities in the bulletin. We have an army of volunteers because we have a system of volunteer care and leadership that made them feel valued, loved, and respected. I was pouring into a team of dedicated leaders that were, in turn, pouring into teams of volunteers. Relationships were being forged, friendships were being nurtured, and spiritual growth was taking place within our ministry. We were more focused on developing people spiritually than we were on making sure our schedules were filled and full. Relationships, time, and love... those were the key ingredients I failed to share with the people I was mentoring.

Just a short time later, I was given the chance to talk to a group of pastors about leading volunteers. I had 30 minutes to tell them everything I knew. I'm sure they came expecting strategies for recruiting volunteers through bulletins and newsletters. Instead I gave them a shift in perspective. I shared with them for 40 minutes (yes, I went over my time) that the key to recruiting and retaining volunteers is relationships.

As leaders, we need to view ourselves in the role of developing people, not merely volunteer managers and schedulers. Instead of looking at potential volunteers with the mindset of "What can you do for me," we need to ask, "What can this ministry do to develop you?" We must realize that our ministry is as much about helping volunteers grow spiritually through their service as it is about the service we will provide to others.

Leading volunteers and focusing on relationships is a risky, messy business. It's easier to manage volunteers- a schedule doesn't talk back. Consider these points:

- Volunteer Managers see people as the answer to their need. Volunteer Leaders develop people and look for areas where they will experience the most personal growth- even if it isn't their ministry's greatest area of need.
- Volunteer managers e-mail duties because it's quick and convenient. Volunteer leaders schedule time over coffee to get personal and talk about what's happening, even though it can be time consuming and overwhelming.
- Being a volunteer manager allows you distance and doesn't require personal investment or further discussion. Being a volunteer leader means investing yourself in a real relationship with volunteers that may make you feel vulnerable and inadequate as you do life together.
- Being a volunteer manager is easy as long as people do what you want them to do. Being a volunteer leader is a commitment toward investing in others and shepherding their spiritual growth. It's a daunting and often overwhelming task that can only be accomplished with a strong connection to the Savior.

Unfortunately the world of church ministry has too many volunteer managers and not enough volunteer leaders. That's why so many ministries are constantly understaffed and struggle to accomplish their mission.

Making the Shift

It is a shift in philosophy and practice to move from a manager to a leader but this shift isn't a magic potion that will have volunteers flooding into your ministry in a matter of days. It's a change in perspective and habits- something that takes time and investment.

Studies have shown it takes a person 21 days to learn a new habit or break an old one and then another 42 days of consistent practice in order for that habit to become a regular part of one's routine and character. Over the next 21 days you'll have the opportunity to develop new leadership skills that will naturally draw people toward serving in your ministry area. You'll have the opportunity to identify and release old, ineffective habits and begin to establish a fresh new approach to leading volunteers. It will be up to you to put those skills into practice in the months that follow and make them become an integral part of your character and interactions with others.

As you dig into this resource, you'll be immersed in an extensive training program that will require you to take an objective look at your skills as a leader and your ministry as a whole. The effectiveness of this training depends on your ability to be completely honest about your own strengths and weaknesses and to let go of personal ownership of your ministry. As you begin, it's essential to step outside your ministry context and start from a fresh point of view. With an open mind, you're ready to begin this three-week journey of volunteer leadership development!

USING THIS GUIDE

Each week we'll focus on a different aspect of volunteer leadership. Six days of the week, you'll read the material and answer the corresponding questions. On the seventh day of each week, you'll have the opportunity to reflect and review what you've learned in the previous lessons. Here's an overview of the next 21 days.

Week One- Attracting Volunteers: Become a Leader Worth Following
> To start things off, we'll take a look in the mirror and focus on character traits that volunteers look for in an effective leader. By changing your approach to leadership, you can set an example that others will want to follow.

Week Two- Recruiting Volunteers: Establish a Ministry worth Joining
> In the second week, we'll evaluate your ministry. You'll have the opportunity to check your vision, motivation, and structure to make sure they not only meet the needs of those you serve, but also provide a healthy environment for volunteers in ministry.

Week Three- Retaining Volunteers: Value Relationships in Ministry
> We'll wrap things up with a study of how to care for volunteers who partner with you in ministry. When volunteers are happy, they are more effective, excited, and they tell others. By valuing relationships over tasks, your volunteers will be compelled to stay, become more invested, and bring others into the ministry.

Remember- you'll get out of this study what you put into it. If one concept seems particularly challenging, you may need to spend more time working through the questions. Take your time and answer thoughtfully, but don't become so bogged down that you get discouraged and quit. Keep pressing on! At the end of these three weeks, you will have completed an honest evaluation of your ministry and leadership skills. This process will take time and attention, but the effort will be worth it! You'll begin to become the kind of leader who naturally attracts volunteers and you'll lead a ministry that people will ask to join.

Volunteer Magnetism, by Anne Bosarge

WEEK ONE—
ATTRACTING VOLUNTEERS:
BECOME A LEADER WORTH FOLLOWING

We need more volunteers... that's the problem in a nutshell. So what do we do? We climb inside the hamster wheel of promotion and recruitment. We continually advertise in the newsletter, place ads in the bulletin, put up help wanted ads in the hallway, pressure parents into serving, learn how to manipulate people with guilt, encourage people who are already overcommitted, and target people who just can't say no. We feel like we are constantly recruiting but we're not getting anywhere! People aren't responding! What's wrong with them? Why weren't they moved to action when we paraded the crying babies through the sanctuary and pleaded for help??!!!

Albert Einstein once said, "Insanity is doing the same thing over and over again and expecting different results." Get off the hamster wheel. Stop recruiting. Stop expecting people to join your ministry using the same tactics that haven't worked in the past. Try something new.

Take a look in your rearview mirror. Who is behind you? If you don't see anyone following, then you're not really leading. If you see a few people in the distance, curious about who you are and what you stand for, learn how to draw them closer. If you look in your rearview mirror and see people walking behind you, desiring to be a part of the things you're connected with, and wanting to learn from your life experiences, you're doing something right.

The first step in successful volunteer recruiting is becoming a leader worth following. As a volunteer leader, you need to be the kind of person that others want to follow because they find value in being near you. They should be able to see the way you love others and the way you value your relationship with God. They should be intrigued by that "something different" about you- something they want to better understand and experience.

This week we'll focus on you and your leadership skills. What can you do to be the type of leader God is calling you to be? Once you put these skills into practice, you'll begin to look in the rearview mirror and see people following you. Then it won't take a creative ad campaign to fill your ministry positions, all it will take is a personal ask to get them to join your ministry journey.

DAY 1- IT STARTS WITH LOVE

*John 15:12 "This is my commandment,
that you love one another as I have loved you."*

It's time to dig in and get started! You probably have a big list of questions you'd like to see answered. What are the best strategies for recruiting volunteers? How do I find the right person for the right job? How do I hold onto the volunteers I have? What do I do if my volunteers leave? And I bet that's just the beginning! Let me give you one simple answer. The first step to solving all your volunteer dilemmas is simple... love. Pure, simple, love. Alright- close the book... you're done. If you only learn one thing about volunteer leadership from this resource, let it be that. Love others.

Jesus spent an incredible amount of time loving others. Consider His approach to volunteer recruitment: first He loved them, then He empowered them. Before He expected anything of His followers, He loved them. Think of Jesus' team of core volunteers (the disciples)- they were fishermen, a tax collector, ordinary uneducated men prone to mistakes, faults, and lapses in faith. None of them could offer Him anything in return. They didn't have incredible communication skills or a knack for leading small groups. They didn't have advanced degrees and certificates to show their potential. He loved them because of who they were, not what they would do for Him. We need to love people in the same way- unconditionally: because of who they are, not what they can do for us or our ministry.

As a leader of volunteers, you are first called to love. Accept other's faults and appreciate their strengths. View them as a masterpiece created by the master craftsman. Don't see them as a potential tool in your ministry toolbox or a missing piece in your program's puzzle, but as a uniquely crafted individual- a child of the King. Ask God to begin to show you His plan for their lives and make it a priority to help them discover their path- regardless of whether or not it benefits your ministry. Become a leader who cares more about other's passions and strengths than your ministry's needs and wants. Start with love.

In the space below, make a list of three people you will intentionally begin to love. Don't limit yourself to people who have something to offer you, but prayerfully seek out who God is leading you to invest in. Then list the ways you will begin to demonstrate that unconditional love. If it truly is more blessed to give than to receive (Acts 20:35), focus on giving love rather than receiving anything in return.

God is calling me to show love to: _____,

_____ and _____ .

Things I value about each of these people:

_____
_____
_____
_____
_____

Ways I will express love toward each of them:

_____
_____
_____
_____
_____

Things I will do to invest in these relationships:

_____
_____
_____
_____
_____

DAY 2- IS "IT" IN YOU?

Philippians 4:9, "Whatever you have learned or received or heard from me, or seen in me- put it into practice. And the God of peace will be with you."

What are some characteristics you are looking for in someone who volunteers in your ministry? Write a description of the perfect volunteer in the space below.

_____
_____
_____
_____

Consider your description and take an honest look at yourself. Do you measure up to your idea of the ideal volunteer? Do you consistently demonstrate these characteristics in your own life? Can others see you not only meeting but exceeding these expectations?

If it's not in you, you can't expect it to be in those you lead. Consistently setting high standards and challenging yourself personally, professionally, and spiritually makes people curious. Hard work, integrity, excellence, and discipline are rare characteristics in today's society. When people see these traits demonstrated in your life, they'll sit up and take notice. They'll recognize the difference and will want to hang out with you. Instead of "recruiting" volunteers for ministry, you'll be able to look behind and see people following who are intrigued by your devotion and eager to see how God is working in your life. These new recruits will desire to be a part of your ministry so they can learn from your life and experiences and be a part of a winning team.

So how do you get "it" in you? Answer the following questions and begin to intentionally build Christian character and spiritual disciplines into your life.

1. What are five character traits you most respect in others?

   _____ _____ _____
   _____ _____

Volunteer Magnetism, by Anne Bosarge

2. How do you plan to challenge yourself to become stronger in those areas? List the trait and a strategy for strengthening your character in that area.

Character Trait	Strengthening Strategy

DAY 3- WORK ETHIC

Matthew 5:41, "If a soldier forces you to carry his pack one mile, carry it two miles."

Circle words that someone would use to describe your effort in ministry:

Good enough	Excellent	Ordinary
Acceptable	Creative	Average
Remarkable	Extraordinary	Energetic
OK	Normal	Different

In Jesus' day it was the right of Roman soldiers to demand favors from citizens- whether it be food or labor. In Matthew 5:41, Jesus said to his followers, "If a soldier forces you to carry his pack one mile, carry it two miles." Even in the face of adversity, Jesus asks us to 'go the extra mile' for people. If we apply this same principle to our work ethic, how does this change the way you approach ministry? Instead of doing just enough to get the job done, how can you go the extra mile in order to show people the exceptional saving power of God's love? Instead of settling for average, how can you push on toward excellence to bring honor to God's almighty name?

So how do you balance the need to excel with the practical limitations of your abilities and time? Here are a few tips and warnings:

1. Perfectionism- While God encourages us to 'go the extra mile', He doesn't expect perfection. Perfectionism stinks of control and independence- two dangerous temptations in the life of a leader. Someone who has given in to the pursuit of perfection has a false sense of control- seeking to manipulate circumstances in order to produce a desired outcome. Your ministry will never be perfect because it's full of imperfect people led by an imperfect person- you! Striving for perfection creates the false sense that it's all up to you- that somehow you should have the ability to control and determine every outcome. God doesn't want us to be in control of every situation and completely independent. He wants just the

opposite from us- to allow Him to be in control and demonstrate complete dependence upon Him!

Where are you tempted to strive for perfection? How is that dangerous to your ministry?

_____
_____

2. Priorities- You can't possibly do *everything* with excellence. If you strive for excellence in all areas, you will quickly burn out. It's essential to be able to determine the areas where God is calling you to go above and beyond in ministry. It's also important to be able to objectively evaluate where God is calling you to step back your efforts. Sometimes, as a leader, the wisest thing you can do is to kill a ministry or program that drains your energy, resources, and volunteer pool. Evaluate what is most important and concentrate your efforts in that direction. Be brave enough to let the rest go. It's better to do a few things well, than many mediocre things.

Where is God calling you to focus your efforts at this time? Are there any areas you need to eliminate in order to accomplish this goal?

_____
_____

3. Check your motivation- We should do more than what is expected of us- not so we will be recognized or glorified, but to demonstrate God's great, extraordinary love to others. When praised for a job well done, always be sure to give God the glory. The next time you are complimented for your pursuit of excellence or a job well done, how can you put the focus back on God?

_____
_____

Volunteer Magnetism, by Anne Bosarge

DAY 4- CHOOSING PEACE UNDER PRESSURE

John 14:27, "I give you peace, the kind of peace that only I can give. It isn't like the peace that this world can give. So don't be worried or afraid."

One of the most attractive qualities of a good leader is the ability to remain calm under pressure. When things go awry, when people disappoint, or when circumstances are beyond your control, it's a great opportunity to choose peace under pressure.

True peace isn't simply a lack of conflict and trouble, it's the ability to remain calm and steady in the midst of difficult, trying circumstances. Peace doesn't depend on outside influences, it's something that comes from within- a quiet confidence that comes from knowing who you are and whose you are.

How can you choose peace in the midst of pressure? How do you prevent yourself from responding to difficult situations in anger and frustration? Below are a few strategies for responding with peace under pressure.

1. **Identify the Source of Peace**- In John 14:27, Jesus said that His peace is very different than the peace this world gives. Many leaders seek peace in cooperative volunteers, successful programs, and approval of others. God's peace is much more than the absence of conflict, it's a joy and contentment that comes from knowing Him intimately and doing His will. God's peace comes from a surrendered heart, completely given over to His will.

   Find a peace promise you can use to help you stay peaceful under pressure. Take a moment to look up the following verses or find one of your own. Memorize it and claim it in times of trouble to help you remember to respond in peace.

Matthew 5:9	John 16:33	Philippians 4:6-7
2 Corinthians 13:11	Mark 9:50	James 3:18

Your Personal Peace Promise:

_____
_____
_____
_____

2. **Find Confidence in your Calling**- When you're certain of your call to ministry, it's much easier to respond to controversy with peace. Take comfort in the fact that God has chosen you and will equip you for the task. Find confidence in knowing that God anticipates your struggles and promises to be with you every step of the way.

   Take a moment to remember your calling. When did you first know God was calling you into ministry? What can serve as a reminder of that calling on your life?

   _____
   _____
   _____
   _____

3. **Put Things in Perspective**- Don't sweat the small stuff. Many times the circumstances that annoy us most don't really matter in the long run. When things go wrong, evaluate the situation- does this affect the ultimate goal, vision, or direction of your ministry? Ask yourself...

   How will I feel about this in 10 minutes?
   How will I feel about this in 10 days?
   How will I feel about this in 10 years?

   If the situation does not have a lasting impact on the effectiveness of your ministry, respond with peace and let it go. Don't allow minor irritants to steal your peace and hi-jack the direction of your ministry.

4. **Relationships over Tasks**- When situations and struggles present themselves, remember that relationships are more important than tasks. The relationship you have with your volunteers should take priority over the tasks that need to be done. If you engage in a conflict over a minor task and damage the relationship with a volunteer, not only will you lose that person's respect and trust, you'll also lose the respect and trust of other volunteers on your team. Your ministry is just as much a ministry to your volunteers as it is to the people you serve.

5. **Find a Way to Grow**- When under pressure, ask yourself if the situation is an obstacle to be overcome or an opportunity for growth. Learn a lesson from every struggle and turn each difficulty into an avenue for growth.

    Think of a situation in your ministry that you often struggle with. Write it in the blank below.

    _____
    _____

    What lesson might God want you to learn from this experience?

    _____
    _____
    _____
    _____

DAY 5- PEOPLE PLEASERS

Colossians 3:23-24, "Whatever you do, work heartily, as for the Lord and not for men, knowing that from the Lord you will receive the inheritance as your reward."

When working and serving in a relationship-rich environment, it's important to keep your own motivations in check. As a leader who is actively developing people, it's very easy for your focus to switch from the mission of the church to pleasing people in the church. Be on the look-out for warning signs that you are a people pleaser.

1. **You crave recognition and are resentful when you don't get it.** By placing an emphasis on man's fleeting admiration, you have given people control of your emotions and self-worth. If things go well in ministry, you feel valuable. If things are difficult, you feel useless. If someone else gets praise you feel you deserve, you become bitter. Man's admiration is temporary. God's admiration is eternal. Shift your perspective- don't seek constant approval from men- bask in God's delight of you. He loves you for who you are- not what you do or the successes you have in ministry.

    Think about how God sees you- not what you do, but who you are. What do you imagine He sees in your character? What do you suppose He loves most about who you are? Stay away from thoughts based on performance- God loves who you are more than what you do for Him!

    _____
    _____
    _____
    _____
    _____

Volunteer Magnetism, by Anne Bosarge

2. **Your programs are directed by people and not by prayer.** People have a million opinions and are usually not shy about expressing them- to your face or behind your back. If you direct programs simply based on the opinions of volunteers or participants, your programs will lack cohesion and focus. You won't see the fruits of your labor because the minute something fails, you abandon ship and look for a suggestion from someone else. Instead of trying to please people, stay true to the vision God gave you for this ministry. Constantly revisit your mission statement and ask God to clarify His calling. Seek His direction and guidance. Trust the opinions of people who have been seeking God's guidance and direction for the ministry.

    Schedule a time to go on a vision prayer retreat, either alone or with a small team of invested volunteers. Take time to pray and listen to God speak to you about the direction and mission of your ministry. Record the date, place, and time of this retreat in the space below:

    _____

3. **You are afraid to fail publically.** Is there a commandment in the Bible that says, "Thou shall not fail"? When God calls you to do something BIG for Him, there is a chance that it will fail. Sometimes failure is needed to build character, narrow the focus of a ministry, and refine the vision. Don't be afraid to admit failure. Just because a program failed, doesn't mean you have failed personally. God uses failure to teach us lessons we would not be able to learn in other ways. Through our failure, He reminds us to depend on Him.

4. **You are easily offended.** When volunteers express a critical opinion, you get angry. When they talk about you behind your back, you feel hurt. When they don't show up, you assume they don't like serving with you. People-pleasers are easily offended. They take everything personally because their sense of self-worth comes from who others believe them to be. God-pleasers are nearly unoffendable. They attempt to see past the hurtful words and identify the cause of a volunteer's frustration. God-pleasers seek to make peace and forgive.

In order to be an effective volunteer-leader, it's vital that you are a God-pleaser and not a people-pleaser. Volunteers are not attracted to ministries that are controlled by the opinions of a select few. People are attracted to a leader who stands firm to what God is calling Him to do. Leaders who seek God first are respected because their volunteers know that God can be trusted.

Pray and ask God to identify any people-pleasing motivations in your life. Realign your passion to His vision. Reconnect with God as the object of your worship and the source of your worth. Choose one of the scriptures below and turn it into a scripture prayer that will help you keep a proper perspective of ministry.

> *Galatians 1:10, "For am I now seeking the approval of man, or of God? Or am I trying to please man? If I were still trying to please man, I would not be a servant of Christ."*
>
> *Romans 12:2, "Do not be conformed to this world, but be transformed by the renewal of your mind, that by testing you may discern what is the will of God, what is good and acceptable and perfect."*
>
> *Matthew 6:33, "But seek first the kingdom of God and his righteousness, and all these things will be added to you."*

_____
_____
_____
_____
_____

DAY 6- COURAGEOUS GOALS

Joshua 1:9, "Have I not commanded you? Be strong and courageous. Do not be afraid; do not be discouraged, for the Lord your God will be with you wherever you go."

One way to be a leader others will follow is to set high goals and consistently meet or exceed them. In ministry, it's important for leaders to take steps of faith- to completely trust God when He asks you to do something that seems beyond your ability. Those you lead need to see you place your faith in Him to help you accomplish courageous goals.

There are a few important things to remember when making and setting courageous goals:

1. **Courageous goals are not foolish goals.** Foolish goals are created out of pride, self-centeredness, and with a lack of spiritual guidance. They tend to test the boundaries of your own power instead of demonstrating the majesty of God's power. On the other hand, courageous goals are birthed from prayer and a connection with God. They are grounded in scripture and often feel just out of reach.

2. **Courageous goals cause you to move outside your comfort zone.** In order to do big things for God, you have to be willing to move outside of what is comfortable and learn to rely on His strength and power. It's when you are operating outside your comfort zone that you have the biggest opportunity for spiritual growth. It's a feeling of inadequacy that brings you to your knees and helps you seek Him more fully.

   Take a moment to consider your comfort zone. Where are you most comfortable in ministry?

   _____
   _____

What tasks, responsibilities, situations challenge your comfort and skills? Where do you think God may be stretching your abilities?

_____
_____

3. **Courageous goals require divine intervention.** These God-given goals are never meant for us to accomplish in our own strength. It's not even possible for us to achieve them on our own! God uses our journey toward these goals to draw us closer to Him. We discover that He is all we need.

4. **Courageous goals should bring glory to God.** At the completion of a courageous goal, be sure to attribute the honor and praise to God. Success carries with it the temptation of pride- taking credit for achievements belonging to God. When you are successful, recognize that the power to complete the goal came not from your own strength, but from God's. Use this as a stepping-stone to spiritual growth and a closer relationship with God- not as a means of building your own self-esteem.

Take time over the next few days to pray about a courageous goal you think God is calling you to- either personally or in ministry. Once you are sure it is God-driven and Bible-based, come back and write the goal in this space.

_____
_____
_____

How does this stretch you as a leader and push you outside your comfort zone?

_____
_____
_____

Volunteer Magnetism, by Anne Bosarge

In what ways will you rely on God's guidance and power as you work toward accomplishing this goal?

_____
_____
_____

After accomplishing the goal, how will you give God the glory for your success? What steps will you take to make sure you don't take the credit?

_____
_____
_____

DAY 7 - REST AND REFLECT

1 Corinthians 11:1, "You must follow my example, as I follow the example of Christ."

You made it through the first week! During the last six days, you've done the hard work of self-evaluation and reflection. You've been able to identify areas of strength and weakness within your character and have made some progress on the life-long journey of becoming more and more like Christ.

An effective and Godly leader constantly seeks to improve and refine his character- to become more and more like Christ. Leaders of volunteers should constantly strive to grow in their knowledge and love of God and others. Take a moment to reflect on the journey you've taken the last week.

What stands out as the most important lesson you've learned?

_____
_____
_____

What concept is most challenging for you?

_____
_____
_____

How have these exercises clarified your calling to ministry?

_____
_____
_____

WEEK 2: RECRUITING VOLUNTEERS: ESTABLISH A MINISTRY WORTH JOINING

Now that you've taken the time to evaluate yourself as a leader, let's go the next step and take time to assess how well your ministry is doing to attract prospective volunteers. Imagine there is a table full of gifts in front of you and you can choose any of them you want. Each one is wrapped a little differently. Some are covered with classic brown paper and a simple twine bow; others are beautifully covered with shiny paper and sparkling ribbons. Some are big; some are small. Some presents look like they required a lot of time and energy, others look like they were wrapped hastily at the last minute. Which present would you choose?

Potential volunteers are faced with a similar experience when choosing a ministry to join. Do they want a big ministry or a small one? Are they looking for something basic and foundational or are they looking for fun and flashy? Because of the way God has uniquely crafted each individual, they are each drawn to different aspects of church ministry. As potential volunteers consider their options, they are looking at the way each ministry is packaged and displayed.

So what does your packaging say about your ministry? Are you all fluff and no substance? Do you have good intentions, but haven't figured out how to effectively communicate it to a wider audience? Do you have a solid foundation, but need some work on how others perceive your ministry? Does the view from outside do an effective job of portraying the vision and mission found on the inside?

This week we'll work on establishing a ministry worth joining. You'll learn how to package your ministry so it will be attractive to people who follow you. They will be able to clearly see your vision, find a path to become involved, and have an opportunity to put their spiritual gifts to work. By spending time on the structure and presentation of your ministry, you'll see followers naturally become ministry partners.

DAY 8- REFINE YOUR VISION

Habakkuk 2:2, "Then the Lord answered me, "Write the vision. Make it clear on tablets so that anyone can read it quickly."

Once you have taken inventory of your personal motivations and character, it's time to evaluate the foundation of your ministry. It's essential that your ministry is on a solid foundation before you invite others to partner with you. This foundation begins with your vision.

God wanted to make sure Habakkuk could communicate His vision for the people in a way that others would be able to share. You need to take the same approach with your ministry. You should wait to hear from God, write it down, and communicate the vision to others in a way that is easily passed on.

Hear from God- Prayerfully consider how to clarify the vision and direction of your ministry by answering the following questions:

Why does your ministry exist? What is unique about your ministry? What's your big vision?

_____
_____
_____
_____
_____

What specific goals do you have? What do you hope to accomplish?

_____
_____
_____
_____
_____
_____
_____

Volunteer Magnetism, by Anne Bosarge

What opportunities do you have for others to partner with you in accomplishing your vision?

_____
_____
_____
_____

Write It Down- Before asking people to join your ministry team, you must be able to clearly communicate God's vision for your ministry. People are attracted to a big vision, clearly defined goals, and specific roles. They want to know you've prayed about it, received direction from God, and have a plan to accomplish the tasks set before you. Organization and unclear direction show people you don't care. Their perception will be, "If you don't care, why should I?"

Take a moment to write down your ministry's vision, goals, and roles. Come back to this each day for a week- adjusting and changing it as God continues to reveal and clarify His vision in your heart.

Vision/Mission Statement (make it short and memorable):

_____
_____

Three goals for accomplishing your vision (make sure they are measurable and have an ending time such as this suggested format- "from x to y by z"):

_____
_____
_____
_____
_____

Ways people can partner with you to accomplish your goals (specific roles and a one sentence job description for each):

_____
_____
_____
_____
_____
_____
_____
_____
_____
_____
_____
_____

Communicate the Vision- Have a plan for sharing your vision, goals, and roles with your existing and potential volunteers. Consistently communicate your vision in written materials and conversation. Remind volunteers of their role in helping your vision become reality. Help them see their role as more than just a simple task- as part of a bigger ministry picture and God's story of redemption. Once your volunteers catch the vision and realize their part in making it happen, they'll share it with other potential volunteers and your ministry will grow.

How will you communicate the vision to your current volunteers to make sure everyone is on the same page?

_____
_____

How will you communicate the vision to new, potential volunteers?

_____
_____

Volunteer Magnetism, by Anne Bosarge

DAY 9- A PLACE FOR EVERYONE

1 Peter 4:10, "As each has received a gift, use it to serve one another, as good stewards of God's varied grace."

God uniquely equipped each of us with gifts and abilities to match the variety of needs in the church and our world. As a ministry leader, it's your responsibility to find a variety of ways for people to participate in His work. Instead of limiting the types of roles in your ministry, think creatively about ways people with different gifts can get plugged in. When you engage a variety of people with different strengths, your ministry becomes more rich and diverse. Take a moment to consider the following spiritual gifts and record possible roles within your ministry that could be filled by someone with that gift.

Gift	Descriptors	Ministry Role
Administration	organization, planning, delegating, directing people, ability to clarify and direct	
Evangelism	personable, open to sharing their story, welcoming to new people	
Exhortation	motivate others to action, show others how to apply truth, counsels, encouraging, practical	
Giving	generous, able to identify a need and moved to meet it, highly motivated to help others, heart for missions	
Mercy	comforting, nonjudgmental, loving, sympathetic, seeks out those who have needs	

Volunteer Magnetism, by Anne Bosarge

Serving	desires to serve by helping others, meets practical needs of others, quick to respond to needs, flexible and willing	
Teaching	communicates truth effectively, enjoys study, creative and imaginative, strives for accuracy	
Prophecy	discernment, helps guide others' choices, not afraid to speak truth	
Shepherding	strong desire to serve God, overseeing the spiritual development of others, burden to see others grow,	
Other Gifts and Talents:		

In addition to matching gifts with service areas, you'll need to consider a volunteer's availability and ability to commit. Due to changing needs in your volunteers' lives, you'll need to have a variety of commitment options and entry points so they can adjust the level of responsibility and commitment.

What levels of commitment do you offer in your ministry?

Owner- A person who owns the vision, is fully-vested, and spends significant time and energy working toward your vision and goals. These are typically people who come to team meetings, volunteer to come to extra events, spend time thinking about the ministry away from church, and are people others look up to. What roles within your ministry are a match for those who want to be owners?

_____
_____
_____

Facilitator- A person who assists by filling a role on a regular basis but doesn't direct the overall vision of the ministry. Facilitators typically serve on a regular basis but prefer to walk in and serve with little advance prep or thought. What roles within your ministry are a match for those who want to be facilitators?

_____
_____
_____

Window Shopper- A person who helps with a one-time special event and is able to catch a vision of what it would be like to serve at a deeper level within the ministry. What roles within your ministry are a match for those who want to be window shoppers?

_____
_____
_____

DAY 10- NEVER ALONE

Ecclesiastes 4:9, "Two people are better off than one, for they can help each other succeed. If one person falls, the other can reach out and help. But someone who falls alone is in real trouble."

Is ministry a lonely place? Do you ever feel like you're doing all the work? God never intends for you to do life or ministry alone. His desire is for you to live in community with Him and with each other. The church is to be an earthly glimpse of Heaven- a diverse community of faith united in worship and truth. By creating a ministry where others have the opportunity to serve and contribute, you're enhancing the community of faith. As you structure your ministry roles, consider the following suggestions.

1. **Identify an Apprentice-** The first step in sharing your ministry with others is to identify an apprentice for each of your roles. Choose someone who possesses some different strengths and weaknesses, so your ministry will develop depth and diversity that will attract more types of people to your ministry. Never do anything alone- be intentional about replacing yourself and train your volunteers to think about replicating themselves.

2. **Adjust Your Expectations**- Some leaders are unwilling to share control because they have a picture in their mind of what the end result should be and the steps by which it should be accomplished. They are unwilling to change their expectations and release control. However, leaders who effectively develop volunteers, see that process as more important than the outcome of the program or event. They are willing to adjust expectations and see that there is more than one way to do ministry. When you share a project with an apprentice, have a general idea of the desired outcome, but be willing to adjust your plans when new ideas arise. Realize that this isn't **your** ministry, it's **God's** ministry.

Volunteer Magnetism, by Anne Bosarge

3. **Push and Pull**- There is a delicate balance when determining how much responsibility is appropriate to give a volunteer. It's important to empower people who are ready to soar, and shepherd people who are unsure. Leaders must know when to give responsibility and how much is just the right amount.

   So how do you know when to push and when to pull? Give a volunteer a small amount of responsibility in a short-term project or one-time event and turn over complete control. Don't micromanage- allow them some ownership and responsibility. Check with them periodically, asking questions about progress and offering help and assistance if needed. If the volunteer is successful and has shown initiative, you'll be able to give them more responsibility next time. If help and guidance was required throughout the project, give them another small short-term project and shepherd them through that process again until they are comfortable taking the lead. There is no magic formula for knowing how much responsibility is too much and how much is not enough. In order to effectively discern what is best for your volunteers, you need to be intentional about spending time together and listening to them.

4. **It's Worth the Time**- "It's just easier to do it myself." Have you ever said that? It's usually a true statement- when you know how to do a task, it's often easier to do it yourself rather than taking time to show someone else how to do it. The problem with that statement is that you fail to develop new leaders when you do it yourself. God desires that everyone find a place to use their gifts in the service of His church. By failing to share opportunities with others, you are hindering them from using their gifts. Raising up leaders is a time-consuming task. If done right, you'll actually spend more time building relationships with volunteers than doing the actual work of ministry. It might make you cringe to think about the investment of time that takes. You may think, "That's not possible! I can't do all the work I have to do now! I can't afford to invest in developing volunteers." If that's true- stop doing so much. Your programs will

never move forward without volunteer support and you'll never have the kind of volunteers you need if you can't invest the time to develop them.

Stop and Think- Identify apprentices for each of your programs, ministries, or responsibilities. If you do not have an apprentice for a certain area of ministry, develop a timeline for developing one.

Ministry Role	Person Responsible	Apprentice	Timeline

Volunteer Magnetism, by Anne Bosarge

DAY 11- HOW TO FISH

Matthew 4:18-20, "While Jesus was walking along the shore of Lake Galilee, he saw two brothers. One was Simon, also known as Peter, and the other was Andrew. They were fishermen, and they were casting their net into the lake. Jesus said to them, "Follow me! I will teach you how to bring in people instead of fish." Right then the two brothers dropped their nets and went with him."

Effective, clear communication is a powerful tool in the tackle box of an expert leader. Knowing who to approach, when to address them, what words to use, and how to communicate your message clearly determines your ability to grow your volunteer team. Jesus got incredible results when He recruited his first volunteers! Consider these points from Jesus' example and how they apply to recruiting volunteers for your ministry.

1. **Jesus sought them out-** He recruited his volunteers in person. He didn't place an ad in the church newsletter, show a funny video on the screen, or put a clipboard with a sign-up sheet in the back of the sanctuary. He went directly to his volunteers and asked them.

    Approach potential volunteers in person. Look them in the eye, engage them in conversation, and show them you care about them personally- begin to build the relationship. A personal ask demonstrates that you have identified something special in their character that matches with the needs of your ministry.

2. **Jesus didn't wait for them to realize their need.** He didn't sit around hoping they would realize their calling to ministry. He took the initiative to ask.

    Don't wait for someone to hear a calling from God before asking them to serve in your ministry. God may be waiting to speak to them through you. Take the initiative to ask boldly with confidence.

3. **Jesus communicated His vision in a clear, concise way.** He didn't say, "I need someone to serve in this role at this time." He offered an opportunity to partner with Him in a life-changing ministry.

   Rehearse the way in which you ask volunteers to serve. Offer an opportunity to use their gifts, not merely fill a timeslot or task. Volunteers are less interested in meeting your needs than in using their gifts to serve God's greater purpose.

4. **Jesus put them to work immediately.** He didn't ask them to join the team and get back to them in a few weeks with more details. Their imaginations were engaged and they were ready to follow. He immediately began to teach and minister to them.

   Once you ask, make sure you have the systems in place for people to begin to serve quickly. If you allow too much time to lapse, they will feel unimportant and unneeded. They're likely to lose interest and not follow through.

5. **Jesus asked friends to serve together.** He invited Peter and Andrew to serve together- He knew that serving is more fun with a friend.

   Get a two-for-one deal by recruiting spouses, parents and kids, or friends into a ministry position together. Encourage your existing volunteers to become recruiters with an "Each One, Ask One" campaign where you challenge each volunteer to invite a friend to join the ministry team and allow them to serve together.

6. **Jesus didn't stress them with the details.** He didn't point out all the commitments and costs up front. He simply asked and they responded to the vision and His call on their life.

   It's important to be very clear and precise with your expectations once volunteers have expressed an interest in joining your ministry. However, the first ask should focus on vision, not details. You want them to join your ministry based on their passion for what you're doing, not based on whether or not it works well with their schedule.

After looking at Jesus' recruiting style, what are some old practices you need to cast off?

_____
_____
_____

Think about your current volunteer needs. What will you say to a potential volunteer who is being invited to join your team?

_____
_____
_____
_____

List 3 people you would like to recruit for your team. Make a plan for inviting them to join your ministry.

1. _____

2. _____

3. _____

DAY 12- TRAINING AND EQUIPPING

2 Timothy 3:16-17, "All scripture is God-breathed and is useful for teaching, rebuking, correcting and training in righteousness, so that the servant of God may be thoroughly equipped for every good work."

God wants us to be "thoroughly equipped" so we can do the work He has called us to. As leaders of volunteers, it's our responsibility to make sure we do everything we can to equip them with the skills to do the job God has called them to. Training and equipping is much more than handing them a book to read or providing them a curriculum to teach.

There are many different methods for equipping volunteers. A great leader equips volunteers in their personal spiritual development, in their specific volunteer role, and in general leadership skills. Make a plan for equipping the volunteers in your ministry.

Ways to equip volunteers in their personal spiritual development:

1. Provide them with a seasonal devotional.
2. Ask them to pray for each other.
3. Encourage them to work one/worship one or make sure they are on a service rotation that allows them regular worship time.
4. Help them keep the Sabbath- refrain from scheduling lots of meetings on Sundays.
5. Encourage them to have a regular quiet time.
6. Ask them to participate in a small group or accountability group.

How will you equip your volunteers in their personal spiritual development?

_____
_____
_____
_____

Volunteer Magnetism, by Anne Bosarge

Ways to equip volunteers in their volunteer roles:

1. Sunday School Teachers/Small Group Leaders- Take the time to train them in how to best use the curriculum.
2. Youth/Children's Ministry- Teach them how to effectively speak to kids and lead a discussion group.
3. Host Team/Ushers- Train them in the importance of setting a good first impression by giving them a week off to visit another church and become a visitor themselves. Ask for their thoughts and opinions later.
4. Spiritual Gift Inventory- Help volunteers discover the way God wired them to serve.

How will you equip your volunteers in their specific role?

_____

_____

Ways to equip volunteers in general leadership skills:

1. Communication Skills- Help them learn how to effectively reach the people they lead.
2. Teaching Techniques- Expose them to different ways to teach.
3. Goal Setting- Take volunteers through your vision planning process.
4. Assessment/Evaluation- Help them assess and evaluate your programs, allow them to be a part of the data collection and interpretation.
5. Management- Read a leadership book together and communicate about discoveries through e-mail or social media.

How will you equip your volunteers in general leadership skills?

_____

_____

Volunteer Magnetism, by Anne Bosarge

DAY 13 - LIMITATIONS OR CREATIVE OPPORTUNITIES?

Philippians 4:13, "Christ gives me the strength to face anything."

How many times have you attended a conference or workshop, heard some incredible ideas presented, and thought, "I can't do that because..." Have you been a part of a committee meeting and heard someone say, "That's not possible because..." We are all limited in some capacity by time, budget, knowledge, expertise, space or other resources. A great leader knows how to see limitations as creative opportunities and structure their ministry to make the most of them. Volunteers are attracted to ministries that overcome problems and make the most of limited resources.

The first step in learning to turn limitations into creative opportunities is to recognize and embrace your resources. Take a moment and consider the resources available to you.

What would you consider limiting factors in your ministry?

_____
_____
_____

Embracing your limitations means that you stop using them as reasons for failure or excuses not to try new things. Ask God to help you creatively overcome those stumbling blocks and turn them into unique advantages- a reason to approach ministry in a new way, with a different direction. It has been said that "necessity is the mother of invention." Unique ministries are often born when it is necessary to think outside the box to creatively overcome a solution.

Here are some guidelines for turning limitations into creative opportunities in your ministry.

1. **Surround yourself with a think tank of problem solvers.** Gather a group of people whose job is to think of creative solutions that take advantage of available resources. Your think tank needs to be a balanced combination of creative thinkers and detail people who can make it happen.

    Who would you invite to be a part of your think tank?

    _____
    _____
    _____

2. **Instead of saying, "We can't do that because..." say, "We can't do that but we can do this."**

    Fill in the blanks with three examples from your list of limitations.

    We can't do _____ but we can do _____.

    We can't do _____ but we can do _____.

    We can't do _____ but we can do _____.

3. **Generate as many ideas as possible.** Think about creative ways to do ministry that highlight your available resources. The more ideas you throw out, the better the chance that you'll find an idea that meets your church's unique needs.

    What are some creative solutions for one of the limitations you listed earlier?

    _____
    _____
    _____

4. **Test it out.** Create a ministry environment that encourages and accepts change. Try out a new idea for a limited time and be willing to change and adapt it until it works for you. If an idea doesn't work, don't take it personally. Your idea is not your identity! Your value isn't in how many successes you have, it's based on who are you are in Christ!

5. **Be open to new and creative ideas from your volunteers.** Allow their voice to be heard. Sometimes the best ideas come from people in the trenches who are able to see things you are unable to see any longer.

DAY 14- REST AND REFLECT

Ephesians 4:11-12, "Christ chose some of us to be apostles, prophets, missionaries, pastors, and teachers, so that his people would learn to serve and his body would grow strong."

Congratulations on making it through the second week! You've taken time to evaluate your ministry and make sure it is structured in a way that will encourage volunteer participation and help them feel effective in their roles. You've refined your vision, clarified your communication, began to develop a system for training and equipping volunteers, and learned to think creatively.

An effective leader constantly seeks to improve and refine the ministry- to make sure it is meeting the needs of both the volunteers who have committed their time and the people it was created to serve. As you continue to refine your ministry's structure, you'll attract new volunteers who see the dedication and care you take to create an environment that helps them serve others.

Take a moment to reflect on the journey you've taken the last week. What stands out as the most important lesson you've learned?

_____

_____

What concept is most challenging for you?

_____

_____

How have these exercises helped you refine and improve your ministry?

_____

_____

WEEK THREE- RETAINING VOLUNTEERS: VALUE RELATIONSHIPS IN MINISTRY

So you have some followers, and ministry partners volunteering in your ministry. Your task is done, right? All your problems solved? Not exactly! That's just the start! Now the real investment begins. In order for people to continue to commit themselves to your ministry, they need to develop relationships, grow spiritually, and feel valued. If you fail to regularly care for volunteers, your ministry becomes a revolving door for frustrated, burned out ministry drop-outs.

Changing your leadership style to attract volunteers and establishing a ministry that is packaged to draw in partners requires a great amount of personal change and initial investment. Once you develop important leadership skills and have an established, well-packaged ministry, it's tempting to sit back and relax - take it easy! People are following and people are joining and your schedule is full. Life is good!

Unfortunately, this is often what happens when leaders fail to realize the importance of volunteer care. When volunteers aren't personally connected to the other people in the ministry, they begin to drop off. They serve less frequently, come late, and leave early. When they don't feel appreciated, they only do the minimum- just what's required of them. When they feel alone and isolated in ministry, they withdraw and fade unnoticed into the background. When they feel overwhelmed by the responsibility and the workload, they work until they reach a point of burnout and leave your ministry in frustration.

Once people have chosen to follow you and partner with you in ministry, be intentional about developing them. Set up a system to care for and appreciate them. Don't let anyone fall between the cracks. Get to know them and invest in their lives. Retaining volunteers takes an enormous amount of time and energy, but the privilege of investing in people's lives and seeing God work through them within your ministry is priceless.

DAY 15-GET PERSONAL

Philippians 2:4, "Let each of you look not only to his own interests, but also to the interests of others."

When you look at volunteers, do you see a means of filling a timeslot or do you see people growing in their relationship with Christ? What's more important to you- making sure volunteers are on time for their scheduled service or helping them have a deep, fulfilling faith in Christ? As a Christian leader, you need to care less about the role and more about developing the person.

Getting personal with people takes time, energy, and intentionality. Try some of the following suggestions for getting personal with your volunteer team.

1. **Conversation-** Take time to serve alongside volunteers. Ask how they feel about their role. Inquire about their family and work. Get to know their passions, hopes, and dreams.
2. **E-mail Check-Up-** Periodically send e-mails, checking on how things are going and asking if there is anything you can do to serve them better. Follow up on any requests or responses- they need to know you sincerely care about how they are doing.
3. **Lovingly Redirect-** If a volunteer is not being successful in his ministry role, lovingly redirect his efforts to a more appropriate role within the church or your ministry.
4. **Challenge Them-** Encourage them to expand their knowledge and spiritual growth through participation in a small group or accountability group. Ask them to commit to regular attendance in worship.
5. **Work One/Worship One-** If your church has more than one Sunday morning service, encourage volunteers to serve during one and worship during the other. If your volunteers are consistently missing worship, offer to release them from their Sunday morning service role so they can regularly attend worship. Their spiritual growth should be more important to you than the role they fill within the ministry.

Volunteer Magnetism, by Anne Bosarge

6. **Prayer Support-** Pray for several volunteers each week. Send a text message or e-mail and ask them to send you prayer requests. Follow up with them during the week if necessary.
7. **Fellowship Events-** Plan events where you have time to talk and fellowship away from church. Don't talk business! Just enjoy the company and get to know each other on a more personal level.
8. **A Day Away-** Take your regular volunteers on a special "Day Away Worship Service" somewhere outside your church building. Set the stage for an intimate worship experience, communion, and prayer service to recharge their batteries and refresh their souls.

After considering some of the options above, make a plan for getting personal with your volunteers. Write down your thoughts below:

_____
_____
_____
_____
_____
_____
_____
_____

DAY 16- APPRECIATE, APPRECIATE, APPRECIATE

1 Corinthians 1:4, "I always thank God for you because of his grace given you in Christ Jesus."

The best way to get new volunteers is to appreciate the ones you've got. Volunteers don't expect to be rewarded for their service but they love feeling appreciated. Taking time to say thanks in fun, creative ways lets them know you care about the impact they make. There are many ways to say thank you, but below are a few suggestions to get your creative juices flowing.

1. **Say it With Food-** Try simple things like baking cookies, serving coffee with fun fixings, fancy chocolates, or holding meetings off-site at a restaurant. Once a year, invite your volunteers to a special appreciation event - a fix-your-own trail mix bar, candy bar, milk-and-cookies event or a hot chocolate and coffee bar.

2. **Blast it on Social Media-** Take advantage of social media outlets like Twitter, Facebook, and Instagram to brag on specific volunteers or to express general thanks for your volunteer force.

3. **Go Old School**- Take time to send hand-written notes or take pictures of your volunteers in action and print them on magnet or photo paper as keepsakes.

4. **Survey Says-** At least once a year, send an anonymous survey to your volunteers and ask for their honest input on your ministry and programs. Anonymous surveys are easily done online through web-based programs such as Survey Monkey (www.surveymonkey.com). Ask specific questions about each program and the feel/vision/style of your ministry in general. When reading the responses, remember that you asked for honest feedback! Don't take it personally! Your personal identity should not be tied to your programs- their opinions are not a personal insult, but an honest assessment of your ministry. Look for any patterns or responses that are repeated, then meet with a volunteer leadership team and make a plan for tweaking and adjusting your programs accordingly. Volunteers feel appreciated when you care about their input.

Volunteer Magnetism, by Anne Bosarge

5. **Spiritual Support-** Provide seasonal Bible readings or devotionals to enhance their spiritual growth.

How you appreciate them doesn't really matter- it's just important that you take the time and energy to express your thanks. Make it a habit to surprise volunteers with small tokens of your appreciation throughout the year. Volunteers who feel appreciated serve longer, more often, with more passion, and are more likely to recruit their friends.

Use these suggestions as a springboard for coming up with ways to appreciate your volunteers. Schedule appreciations on a quarterly basis. Write a method of appreciation for each season in the space below. Set a date and put it on your calendar so it becomes a priority.

Spring	
Summer	
Fall	
Winter	

Volunteer Magnetism, by Anne Bosarge

DAY 17- BUILDING TEAM SPIRIT

Romans 15:5-6, "May the God of endurance and encouragement grant you to live in such harmony with one another, in accord with Christ Jesus, that together you may with one voice glorify the God and Father of our Lord Jesus Christ."

People want to be on a winning team. If you are having difficulty recruiting new volunteers, check your team spirit and unity. Seeing themselves as a part of a team enables volunteers to clarify their vision, feel a part of something bigger than themselves, and fosters a spirit of unity- as you all work together toward a common goal.

We've all played team games and done trust exercises, but teamwork usually happens in much more subtle, intentional ways. Below are a few strategies for turning your volunteers into a unified, motivated team.

1. **Clarify the Vision**- Remember the vision and goals we emphasized earlier? Well, having a vision is great, but making sure your volunteers own it is the key. Repeat your vision over and over- in printed material, e-mails, and in your verbal communications. Say the same thing in different ways so volunteers do more than memorize a catchy phrase, but make it become the driving force in their ministry service.

    What are some creative ways to communicate your ministry's vision and purpose? Write three different examples below:

    _____
    _____
    _____

2. **Define the Roles**- A team functions best when all the players know and understand their roles. Make sure your roles and expectations are clearly defined and volunteers know how their role contributes to the overall effort of the team. Create job descriptions and post them in a visible spot so volunteers will be on the same page.

Volunteer Magnetism, by Anne Bosarge

3. **Listen-** Make sure all members of your team feel valued and know their opinion is important to you. That doesn't mean you have to act on each opinion that is expressed, but you need to give each volunteer the chance to express thoughts and voice concerns. When listening, don't get defensive, interrupt, or take it personally. Take what they say as their opinion and consider whether or not it has merit.

4. **Establish Trust-** Be trustworthy, reliable, and dependable. Your volunteer team needs to know they can trust that you'll do what you say you'll do. They need to see you following through as a leader. Be fair and value each volunteer's role.

5. **Be Enthusiastic-** Every good team needs a cheerleader who encourages, praises, and recognizes each player's effort. As a leader, you can be that cheerleader. Your enthusiasm determines the energy level of your team. If you are excited about your vision and accomplishing your goals, they will be too. If you encourage your team, they will respond by encouraging each other.

6. **Relationship over Rules-** Volunteers need rules and structure to help them stay organized and effective, but don't let the rules and structure become more important than your relationship with the team. Allow time for them to communicate with each other from time to time. Allow time for them to talk and relate to each other during meetings. Your relationship with them is important, but it's just as important for them to have a healthy relationship with each other.

7. **Collaborate-** Approach team meetings with a spirit of collaboration. Realize that you don't have all the answers and that there is something you can learn from each person on your team. When your

volunteers contribute to creating structure, programs, or planning, they feel a sense of ownership and become more invested in the team.

What are some ways you can build teamwork and foster unity in your volunteer team?

_____
_____
_____
_____

What are some things that are keeping you from a true sense of unity?

_____
_____
_____
_____

DAY 18- FLEXIBILITY

Ecclesiastes 3:1, "Everything on earth has its own time and its own season."

It's important to recognize that volunteers aren't going to stay in the same ministry role forever. In fact, sometimes it's dangerous if they do! As people move through different seasons in their lives, their level of availability and investment will need to change. Effective ministries have a flexible system that allows volunteers to change and adjust as their needs dictate and wise leaders allow volunteers to feel the freedom to move and adjust their roles.

How do you know when to give more responsibility and when to let go? Here are some indicators that your volunteers might be ready for a change.

1. **There has been a significant change in their lives.** The death of a loved one, change in job, personal difficulties, and sickness are just some of the many things that can affect your volunteers' investment. Quitting a high-pressure job may free up more time to volunteer. A period of personal difficulty may require a step back in commitment. Be on the look-out for what's happening in their lives and help them identify when it's time to make a change.

2. **They are not happy with their current role.** Before you quickly offer to move them or adjust their responsibilities, make sure you take time to consider their grievance. Is their unhappiness a result of a larger problem in the ministry, an issue with your leadership style, or has something happened within them that makes their current role a bad fit for them right now? An unhappy volunteer is a warning sign to take action. A wise leader is able to get to the heart of the matter and figure out if it's the ministry, his leadership, or the volunteer's situation that needs to be adjusted.

3. **They are inconsistent- you can no longer count on them.** Volunteers should love where they serve and look forward to being a

Volunteer Magnetism, by Anne Bosarge

part of your ministry. Their excitement and energy should be contagious to all who are around. If they are not reliable or have trouble committing, you may need to encourage them to make a change.

Do you have any volunteers exhibiting those warning signs? Let's explore what to do next.

1. **Have a conversation-** Don't assume you know what's happening in the lives of your volunteers. Care enough to take the time to ask. Remember- relationships are more important than tasks! When you value your volunteers, you will invest the time necessary to find out what's going on in their lives and identify the best environment for them to serve.

   Is there someone you need to have a conversation with right now? Write their name below and schedule a time to talk.

   _____
   _____

2. **Change the scenery-** One way of caring for burnt out volunteers is to change their scenery. Move them from one role to another one- either of more or less investment, depending on the circumstances. Some volunteers need to be challenged- they like change. A change of scenery could be working with a different group of people, in a different location, or in an alternate role in the same ministry setting. It can also mean moving to a completely different ministry within your church. Developing volunteers means that you care more about finding the right place for them to fit than whether or not your ministry is being served. There should be no ministry competition!!

   How can you offer people a change of scenery within your ministry? Name two ways below.

   _____
   _____

3. **Help them Focus-** Many people who are drawn to volunteer in ministry settings, do so because they just can't say no. They end up overcommitted to multiple ministries and are spread too thin. If you see a volunteer who is struggling and serving in multiple ministries within your church, coordinate with the leaders of other ministries and help that volunteer discover her passion and gifts. One fully committed and focused volunteer in your ministry is far more valuable than five who can't fully devote themselves to the mission and purpose of the ministry.

   Are there people on your volunteer team who would benefit from a conversation about focus? Write their names below and plan a time to talk with them.

   _____
   _____

4. **Offer a Leave of Absence-** If they are going through a change in life where they need to focus their efforts and energy in another direction, but are hesitant to leave the ministry, offer a leave of absence. Agree on a set time period for them to step away from their ministry role and commit to checking back with them on a certain date. Taking a leave of absence will often provide clarity. Volunteers will either be able to come back renewed and refreshed or be able to leave the ministry with peace of mind.

   Are there people on your volunteer team who may need a leave of absence? Write their names below and plan a time to talk to them.

   _____
   _____

5. **Letting Go-** Sometimes it's time for volunteers to move on. No one was created to do the same thing year after year. As volunteers grow and mature, their abilities, passion, and commitment levels should change. This is a natural part of helping develop people spiritually! It

may be time for them to move out of one ministry setting and into another. God might be prompting them to revamp another struggling ministry outside your church or to start their own ministry. He may need them to devote more time to family or another area of their life. Whatever the reason, leaders who are passionate about developing volunteers are willing to let go and allow volunteers to leave with dignity, grace, and a feeling of deep gratitude for a job well-done.

When it's time to say goodbye- here are some tips for doing it with compassion.

1. Have a brief exit interview in person or by e-mail. Ask questions like…
    a. What was the most satisfying thing about serving in this ministry?
    b. What was the least satisfying thing?
    c. Did you feel like a valuable part of the team?
    d. What could we have done to better support you as a volunteer?
    e. Would you recommend this volunteer role to your friends? Why or why not?
2. Recognize their contribution. Everyone wants to know they've made an impact. Specifically recognize contributions that volunteers have made to your ministry and thank them for their service.
3. Listen, listen, listen. When volunteers leave out of frustration, they need to vent somewhere and the best place for them to vent is with you! Be compassionate, ask them for advice and help in addressing issues within the ministry, and absorb their frustrations and anger. It's much better for them to have the ability to express it to you, than it is for them to express it using social media, to their friends, or in the community.
4. Allow for a brief period of transition. If you've created an environment of apprenticeship (Day 10), there should be someone ready to step up and into the ministry role. This transition time

helps keep the ministry running smoothly and gives volunteers a level of comfort with the change.

In the space below, create a plan for how you will transition someone out of your ministry. What will you do first? What things are important to keep in mind? How will you help them leave with a positive impression?

DAY 19- LIGHTEN UP!

Proverbs 15:13, "A happy heart makes the face cheerful."

Ministry is serious stuff! It's all about working together to change lives and impact our world with the love of Jesus. It's a heavy responsibility that takes a lot of hands and even more hours. There is no greater mission in the world and our success or failure can affect people's lives for eternity. It's the most important job anyone could ever do!

BUT… it's also meant to be full of joy, excitement, possibility, and fun. Successful leaders have the ability to help volunteers balance the gravity of their mission with a healthy dose of enthusiasm and humor. Everyone wants to find enjoyment in life- help them discover joy through serving in your ministry. There are many ways to keep your volunteers happy and engaged, but a few suggestions are listed below.

1. **Develop a sense of community and family.** Give volunteers the space and time to interact and get to know each other on a personal level. Over time, they'll not only look forward to doing the work of ministry, but they'll also look forward to spending time with each other and deepening those friendships away from the ministry setting.
2. **Offer time for them to interact at social events or church functions.** Instead of another meeting, have a party with fun games that help people get to know each other. Encourage your ministry team to attend church functions together.
3. **Laughter really is the best medicine.** Did you know that laughter lowers blood pressure, gives your muscles a workout, increases blood-flow through the heart, increases oxygen to the brain, reduces stress hormones, increases memory and learning, and improves alertness and creativity? By sprinkling your meetings and ministry settings with humor, you're giving your volunteers a physical and emotional boost! You'll engage their imaginations and spark their enthusiasm.
4. **Give them a VIP backstage pass to ministry.** Don't you love to feel like an insider? To be able to peel back the curtain and see what's

happening behind the scenes? Let your volunteers be the first to hear updates and news from you. Involve them in some of the planning and decisions. Allow them to feel the excitement of change and the momentum created by successful planning and execution.

5. **Go viral.** Did you know enthusiasm is contagious? Are you excited and passionate about what's happening? Is your joy visibly noticeable? Make sure to demonstrate the energy you desire to see in your volunteers. If you do, they won't be able to resist catching a bit of your passion every time they're with you.

6. **Be surprising.** It's great to have a routine and a schedule, but memories are made through fun unexpected surprises. On the spur of the moment, do something fun for your volunteers to show them you care. Send them a funny note or e-mail during the week that has nothing to do with ministry. Invite them for lunch or coffee. Sprinkle your relationships with surprises so there's just enough unpredictability to spark their interest and keep them coming back for more.

7. **Don't mistake sarcasm for humor.** Occasional light sarcasm is funny. Constant sarcasm can be demotivating. Tame your sarcastic wit and know when it's appropriate to use it. Unless people know you really well, it's hard to know how to take a sarcastic person.

Take time to consider how you can lighten up your ministry with intentional fun. Record some ways you can alter your normal schedule to allow for fun at various times: at a meeting, while serving, and during the week.

_____
_____
_____
_____
_____
_____

Volunteer Magnetism, by Anne Bosarge

DAY 20- DIVIDE AND CONQUER

Mark 3:13-14, "Jesus went up on a mountainside and called to Him those He wanted, and they came to Him. He appointed twelve that they might be with Him and that He might send them out to preach."

Do you have more volunteers than you can handle? Are you overwhelmed with the task of serving your volunteers? If so, it's time to divide and conquer! If you've grown so large that you're not able to care for your volunteers anymore, update your structure and develop levels of leadership to ensure that your volunteer team will continue to grow and thrive.

In order to effectively care for your volunteer force, set up a leadership team whose job it will be to develop a relationship with volunteers and handle scheduling, responsibilities, and encouragement for smaller groups. Jesus invested time with a few dedicated followers- his disciples. He taught them, cared for them, and helped them develop the leadership skills they needed to serve others. Your leadership team should be a small group of leaders in whom you'll invest your time, energy, and resources as you train them to lead and care for other volunteers.

When establishing a leadership team, keep the following guidelines in mind:

1. **Picking the Team-** Make sure you choose people who share your vision, have the ability to relate well to people, and are dedicated. Your volunteers will only be as good as your leadership team so make sure you select people who demonstrate the characteristics you'd like to see in your volunteers.
2. **Structure**- Each person on the leadership team should be responsible for the oversight of no more than 15 volunteers. Any more than that and you'll need to divide and conquer again!
3. **Relationships**- Your leadership team needs to be in regular contact with the volunteers they serve. They need to be "people in the trenches" who serve alongside other volunteers, but take an extra interest in developing and encouraging other volunteers.

Volunteer Magnetism, by Anne Bosarge

4. **Meetings**- Regular meetings are crucial for those who have committed to serving on a leadership team. Use your meetings to share your vision, plan for the future, and train your leaders.
5. **Investment**- Be intentional about caring for these leaders spiritually, investing in their lives personally, and modeling how you would like them to treat those whom they are shepherding.

How is your current volunteer structure working? Where could you improve?

_____
_____
_____

What is your ratio of volunteers to leaders?

_____

Who are some people you'd like to raise to a leadership role?

_____
_____
_____

How do you plan to begin and implement a leadership team? Write an action plan and timeline below.

_____
_____
_____
_____
_____
_____
_____
_____
_____
_____

Volunteer Magnetism, by Anne Bosarge

DAY 21- REST AND REFLECT

Acts 20:28, "Look after yourselves and everyone the Holy Spirit has placed in your care. Be like shepherds to God's church. It is the flock that he bought with the blood of his own Son."

You've made it through the last week of this evaluation process! During this week, you've taken time to consider the way you lead volunteers and hone your people skills. You've been able to develop the tools to motivate and lead people not only within a ministry setting, but toward a deeper relationship with others in your church.

As you continue to develop people, you'll find more and more that it's less about the task and more about the way serving draws us closer to Christ. This knowledge will help you keep a proper perspective of ministry and enhance the way you relate to all people- whether or not they are volunteers.

Take a moment today to reflect on the journey you've taken this week.

What stands out as the most important lesson you've learned?

_____
_____
_____

What concept is most challenging for you?

_____
_____
_____

How have these exercises helped you refine and improve your ability to lead others?

_____
_____
_____

CONGRATULATIONS!

Congratulations! You've reached the beginning! After three weeks, you've begun the incredible journey of developing people and leading volunteers. You have a new outlook on what it takes to get off the hamster wheel of recruiting volunteers and realize the time, relationship, and love it takes to develop people. This is the start of a new chapter of leadership for you in ministry!

In order to turn your new skills into habit, you'll need to put what you've learned over the last 21 days into practice for 42 more days. Revisit and reread the chapters in this book, prayerfully consider your leadership style and ministry setting. Ask God to continue to develop you into the leader He has called you to become.

You are now equipped with a holistic way of looking at volunteer leadership. I wish I could say that now you know everything there is to know about leading volunteers. I wish I could say that your ministry will never experience volunteer highs and lows. I can't. But you now have the basic tools you need to get started on a new path in ministry! Never stop developing your leadership skills. Always evaluate and assess your ministry to discover how it can change and grow to include more and more volunteers. Constantly seek new ways to appreciate and develop the volunteers under your care. Recognize that each of your volunteers has something to teach you- be open to learning new life lessons. The time you spend with them will never be wasted. The investments you make developing personal relationships will provide bigger dividends than you can ever imagine.

Rejoice that you've completed this book! But be even more excited about where this shift in perspective will take you and your volunteers on your ministry journey.

Made in the USA
Charleston, SC
10 January 2015